L. E. Stock,

Ottawa,

November, 1987.

THOMAS ARCHER

Architect of the English Baroque

Architectural Monographs: I

Monmouth House, Soho Square

MARCUS WHIFFEN

THOMAS ARCHER

ARCHITECT OF THE ENGLISH BAROQUE

Hennessey & Ingalls, Inc.
Los Angeles, California
1973

This book was originally published in 1950 under the title
Thomas Archer by Art and Technics, London, as No. 3 in their
series *Architectural Biographies*.

ISBN 0-912158-23-9

LC 72-93734

CONTENTS

ILLUSTRATIONS IN THE TEXT

THE PLATES

INTRODUCTION

WHEN the republication of this book was first proposed, my feelings were mixed. Of course it is gratifying to an author to learn that there is a demand for something he wrote more than twenty years ago; on the other hand, the literature of English architecture has grown so much since then that it was hard to believe that as a study of a major architect the book would not, on a rereading, be found to be altogether insufficient and out-of-date. Insufficient it undoubtedly is, in that Archer's work deserves a more detailed presentation and a more thorough analysis than is attempted in it. Yet not so much has been added to our knowledge since it was first published that it cannot be updated, so far as matters of fact are concerned, with a summary of such discoveries as have been made.

On the biographical side, the most important relate to Archer's European travels. It used to be assumed that he set out on these immediately after going down from Oxford — that is, in 1689. Dr Peter Murray, however, found that he was issued a travel pass to go to Holland in January 1690/91,[1] and Dr S. Lang followed this up with the information that he had signed his name as a visitor in the books of the University of Padua the following December.[2] As Dr Murray has pointed out, the war with France meant that Archer must have travelled to Italy via Germany and Switzerland or the Tyrol, and this could have given him first-hand knowledge of the first phrase of German and Austrian Baroque, echoes of which have been detected in his work by more than one critic. (*Pace* Dr Murray, the Wrest pavilion still looks to me more like a directional, Baroque version of Michelangelo's S. Giovanni dei Fiorentini than a variation on the theme of Georg Dientzenhofer's pilgrimage church at Waldsassen; it is surely significant that Michelangelo's engaged columns have painted counterparts in the decorations by Louis Hauduroy in the pavilion.)

1

An addition to be made to Archer's *oeuvre* on the authority of H. M. Colvin's *Dictionary of English Architects 1660-1840* (1954) is the remodelling of Aynho Park, Northants, in 1707-11, with tabernacle frames as Borrominesque as anything in England. Mr Colvin suggests also that Archer designed the monument in Rous Lench church, Worcs, to Sir Francis Rous, which was erected in 1719 by

Aynho Park, Northamptonshire: window in forebuilding.

the executors of Lady Frances Rous, who was the architect's sister. The attribution to him of a more important work, Bramham Park, has been greatly strengthened by Mr Geoffrey W. Beard's discovery of two payments to 'Mr Archer' in Robert Benson's account at Hoare's Bank; made in 1699 and 1700, they show that the house was begun some ten years earlier than used to be thought.[3] Another attributed work that must now be redated, though in the other direction, is the remodelling of Monmouth House. Ms Marie Draper has shown that this was done, or at least begun, for Sir James Bateman, who purchased the house from the Duchess of Monmouth in 1717.[4]

An attribution that seems less firm than it did is that of Addiscombe House; one notes that Mr Kerry Downes, who allowed the possibility of Archer's authorship of the design in his *Hawksmoor* (1959), does not mention him in connection with the

2

house in his *English Baroque Architecture* (1966). And in the latter book Mr Downes shows reason to believe that Kingston Maurward may have been designed by John James. However, the only buildings appearing in the illustrations in this volume that should certainly be taken from Archer are Chicheley Hall and the chancel of Chicheley parish church. Mr J. M. Tanner has shown that Chicheley Hall was designed and built in 1720-25 by Francis Smith of Warwick.[5] Although not a work of Archer, it may still be held to merit inclusion as an exceptionally distinguished example of the adoption of his style by a prominent builder-architect.

Marcus Whiffen
Arizona State University, Tempe
September 1972

NOTES

1. P. Murray, letter to the editor, *The Architectural Review*, Vol. CXXII, p. 88.

2. S. Lang, 'English Architects and Dilettanti in Padua.' *The Architectural Review*, Vol. CXXII, p. 344.

3. G.W. Beard, letter to the editor, *Country Life*, Vol. CXXIV, p. 1421.

4. M.P.G. Draper, 'The Great House in Soho Square,' *Country Life*, Vol. CXXXIV, pp. 592-593.

5. J.M. Tanner, 'The Building of Chicheley Hall,' *Records of Bucks*, Vol. XVII, pp. 41-48.

ACKNOWLEDGMENTS

The author and publishers are much indebted to the following for permission to reproduce illustrations:

The Provost and Fellows of Worcester College, Oxford: drawings, pp. 28, 29. The Trustees of the British Museum: engravings, pp. 37 (redrawn), 64, 69, 81, 84; drawings, pp. 72, 73; letter, pp. 93, 94. The Earl of Portsmouth: paintings, p. 62 (upper photo by A.C. Cooper; lower photo by Country Life). Country Life: plans, pp. 39, 40; photos, pp. 62 (lower), 78, 79, 86, 87, 88, 89. Chatsworth Estates Company: drawings p. 49; photo, p. 82. Messrs B.T. Batsford: photo of drawing, p. 55. The National Buildings Record: photos, pp. 54, 66, 67, 70, 71, 74. Mr A.F. Kersting: photos, pp. 63, 64. Mr W.A. Clark: photos, pp. 76 (upper), 90, 91. Mr Edward Yates: photo, p. 92.

The plates on pp. 64 and 81 are photographs kindly lent by Mr H.B. Leather. The photographs on pp. 2, 50, 51, 53, 56, 57, 59, 77, and the lower photograph on p. 76, are by the author.

FOREWORD TO THE FIRST EDITION

THE most comprehensive published account of Thomas Archer has hitherto been my own article in *The Architectural Review* for November 1943. Since then a good deal of new material has been brought to light—much of it (as a glance through the footnotes of the present volume will show) by Mr Howard Colvin. While I have acknowledged my indebtedness to the published writings of Mr Colvin and others in the relevant places, I owe to Mr. Colvin a special debt for the very generous way in which he supplied information from his own private notes. In particular he drew my attention to Addiscombe House and to the possibility of Bramham Park having been designed by Archer; perhaps even more important, he told me of the existence of the early plan for Hurstbourne Priors at Worcester College.

Finally, perhaps I should say here that I am quite aware of the arguments for and against including attributed as well as documented works in a monograph on an eighteenth-century architect, and that it seems to me that in the case of an architect of so marked an individuality as Archer's the pros far outweigh the cons.

I

THE MAN

THOMAS ARCHER was one of the leading architects of the English Baroque. Quite a short while ago to have said so would have sounded, in English ears, doubtful praise; for in England 'baroque' remained a term of abuse, or at least of disparagement, long after art-historians on the Continent had given it an exact meaning as a purely descriptive one. Moreover, it would hardly have been allowed that there was such a thing as an *English* Baroque. The buildings of Sir John Vanbrugh and Nicholas Hawksmoor were generally regarded as isolated and on the whole regrettable episodes inconveniently dividing the supposedly more indigenous architecture of Wren from the supposedly purer taste of the Palladianism which won the field in the 1730s; Archer was a mere amateur who (as Horace Walpole had put it) 'seemed to think that Vanbrugh had delivered the art from shackles, and that he might build whatever seemed good in his own eyes'.

Today all that is changed. So far as the adjective baroque is concerned, the wheel has come full circle and it is often enough used to describe things to which it cannot properly be applied—and on occasion to cover sins which are really in need of more effective concealment. As for the existence, in architecture, of an English Baroque, it is now recognized that the designs of Vanbrugh, Hawksmoor and Archer, of Wren in his last period, and of numerous lesser men, can be grouped under no other title.

Archer, as will emerge, was in his works at once the least English and the most baroque of the four architects named. But before examining those works let us see what is known of his life.

9

One of the things that is not known is the precise date of his birth; nor is that of his baptism. The most one can say, on the evidence of the record of his matriculation from Trinity College, Oxford, which shows that he was 17 on June 12, 1686,[1] is that he must have been born between June 12, 1668, and June 13, 1669—although if one is to believe the statement of his not altogether accurate epitaph at Hale that he was 74 on May 22, 1743, one may advance the latest possible date by three weeks. He was the youngest son of Thomas Archer of Umberslade in Warwickshire, a country gentleman who became a colonel in the Parliamentary army but subsequently resigned his commission and retired abroad till the Restoration, and his grandfather was Sir Simon Archer, an antiquary to whom Dugdale, in his monumental work on Warwickshire, acknowledges his indebtedness. His eldest brother, Andrew, succeeded to Umberslade in 1685, and between ten and fifteen years later rebuilt the Hall (probably *not* to Thomas's design). In 1693 it was observed of the Archers, in a survey made probably with a view to a marriage settlement, that 'by the Report of all, this Family have lived prudently as well as plentifully'.[2] In 1747 Andrew Archer's son— that is, the architect's nephew—was created Baron Archer of Umberslade.

Such was Thomas Archer's family background. The events of the first thirty-six or thirty-seven years of his life—of the first half of it, in fact—are to say the least obscure, although he may, as we shall see, have designed one or two buildings before the end of that period. His epitaph provides the information that he remained at Trinity three years and afterwards spent four years abroad—what would not the student of his architecture give to know something about his travels! It also tells us that his first wife was Eleanor, the only daughter and heir of John Archer of Welford, Berkshire, and Theydon Gernons, Essex, and that she died of smallpox less

[1] Foster, *Alumni Oxonienses.*

[2] Quoted by Philip Styles, 'Sir Simon Archer 1581–1662', *Dugdale Society Occasional Papers*, No. 6, 1946.

10

than a year after their marriage; the Welford registers record her burial there on December 29, 1703.[1] The next event in Archer's life which can be dated at all closely is his appointment, on or shortly before February 6, 1705,[2] to the post of Groom Porter at the court of Queen Anne. It was an event of the greatest importance to him, giving him as it did both a recognized position at court, with all the desirable connections that implied, and an assured income (which Luttrell, the annalist, put at £1,000 a year).

But what was this somewhat inelegantly named office? In the Middle Ages the Groom Porter's chief duty had been to provide furniture for the royal residences; and that this side of the business had not altogether lapsed by Archer's day is shown by a memorial, dated March 9, 1705, in which he petitions for the restoration of certain privileges in this connection.[3] But furniture included dice, and by the seventeenth century the Groom Porter had become the licenser of gambling places throughout the kingdom, with the right of keeping his own gaming tables in the Christmas season and during Epiphany, and the arbiter of disputes concerning wagers. The warrant for Archer's re-appointment on the accession of George II[4] specifies the places under his 'Care and Over sight' as 'Common Billiards Tables, Common Bowling Grounds, Dicing Houses, Gaming Houses and Common Tennis Courts, etc.'. We find Archer being appealed to in his capacity of arbiter in 1714 in a letter from Lord Raby (later the Earl of Strafford),[5] who writes: 'Permit me to trouble you Sir with a question as Groom Porter, which is Master and judge of all games and wagers, can a man win a wager of any consequence if he is sure of it beforehand?'—the particular example

[1] I am much indebted to the Rev Charles E. Hardy, rector of Welford cum Wickham, for examining the registers for me.

[2] N. Luttrell, *A Brief Historical Relation of State Affairs*, Vol. V, p. 516.

[3] Historical Manuscripts Commission, *Manuscripts of the Duke of Portland at Welbeck Abbey*, Vol. VIII, p. 173.

[4] British Museum, Add. MS: 36, 127. f. 157.

[5] British Museum, Add. MS: 31, 141. f. 169.

being that of a man who wagered that the Lord Lieutenant of Ireland had power to grant a certain commission when he had such a commission in his own pocket. As for the Groom Porter's own gaming tables, several writers have left accounts of visits to them; one from the time of Archer's own tenure of the office is Lady Cowper's, dated January 6, 1715:

> This was Twelfth Night, and such a Crowd I never saw in my life. My Mistress and the Duchess of Montague went halves at Hazard and won £600. Mr Archer came in great Form to offer me a place at the Table; but I laughed, and said he did not know me if he thought I was capable of venturing two hundred guineas at play—for none sit down to the Table with less.[1]

Archer's appointment as Groom Porter nearly coincides with the earliest architectural work that is known for certain to be his, the north wing of Chatsworth; in 1707 he was remembered in the Duke of Devonshire's will to the tune of £200, 'in acknowledgement of his favour and his care and trouble touching the building of my house'[2]—a bequest which seemed worthy of mention to the younger John Bridges writing to Sir William Trumbull four days after the Duke's death.[3] The next dateable event in Archer's life was his appointment, in September 1711, as one of the Commissioners to administer the Act of Parliament for building 'fifty new churches in and about the cities of London and Westminster and the Suburbs thereof'.[4] His activities under this Act included the design of two of his finest buildings—St John's, Westminster and St Paul's, Dept-

[1] *Diary*, quoted by E. B. Chancellor, *The Lives of British Architects*, p. 198.

[2] F. Thompson, *A History of Chatsworth*, p. 70.

[3] Historical Manuscripts Commission, *Manuscripts of the Marquess of Downshire*, Vol. I, p. 851.

[4] For the architectural results of this Act see H. M. Colvin, 'Fifty New Churches', *The Architectural Review*, Vol. CVII, pp. 189–96. Archer was one of the signatories of the report dated December 18, 1711, in which the Commissioners stated that they had found their lack of power to contract with proprietors of suitable sites a great obstruction. (H.M. Stationery Office, in continuation of the reports of the Historical Manuscripts Commission, *The Manuscripts of the House of Lords*, 1710–12, Vol. IX, p. 176.)

ford—and the provision of a survey of a site in the Green Park which had been suggested for one of the new churches but was turned down by the Queen.[1]

Archer's appointment as a Commissioner under the church-building Act of 1711 was due to Robert Harley, Lord Oxford. Eighteen months later, in March 1713, we find Archer applying to Oxford for the post of Comptroller of the Works in place of Vanbrugh (who lost it for political reasons) in a long and interesting letter.[2] After explaining the purpose of the office as 'a check on the workmen and the Board itself, and also as an assistance to the Surveyor' he suggests that it is now more necessary than ever, owing to the great age of the present Surveyor (Sir Christopher Wren), and alleges that frauds and abuses are so great that

> no Queen of England can ever undertake a building worthy of the Crown (though the Palace lies now in ashes) unless some remedy be found to check these proceedings, and I can find no other than putting some men of probity versed in building into the place now vacant that shall not be afraid to oppose the practice of that Board and, if outvoted, to give your Lordship an account in what the Crown is abused. The sum of money that passes there is neither so inconsiderable nor the building of a Palace (which must be sooner or later) such a trifle, as not to deserve your Lordship's consideration, and I believe the placing a proper person here may in time beget such a reform as to deserve £190 per annum, which is allowed.

Archer goes on to refer to his work on the Commission for Churches ('I hope I have been no useless Commissioner, and that the models and designs I have made . . . have not betrayed my ignorance'), and then writes:

> What I have done for the Duke of Shrewsbury [at Heythrop] meets with such general applause and gives him such satisfaction

[1] See letter from Archer to the Earl of Oxford dated May 15, 1713, Historical Manuscripts Commission, *Manuscripts of the Duke of Portland at Welbeck*, Vol. V, p. 291.

[2] Historical Manuscripts Commission, op. cit., Vol. X, p. 145.

that I can desire no better than that your Lordship would take his opinion. . . . The model I had the honour of showing the Queen for a stair to ascend Windsor Terrace with coaches is such an invention as alone would deserve so poor a post as this.

But without insisting on my own merit which may be much inferior to others, the losses I have sustained in my own office [of Groom Porter] by this late Act of Parliament and which I, as the Queen's servant, am obliged to obey whilst all others reap the profit I used to receive, and the losses of so many *twelfth-nights*, one of which was never omitted before, are sufficient arguments to entitle me to your Lordship's favour, and to this post . . . .

Archer's application for the Comptrollership was supported by Shrewsbury, in a letter to Oxford written in Paris eleven days later.[1] 'I think myself obliged,' he wrote, 'as much in respect to her Majesty's service, as in Justice to Mr Thomas Archer, to acquaint you that, impartially speaking according to my skill, he is the most able and has the best genius for building of anyone we have, and by my own experience dare assure you he is so perfectly honest that I am certain the Queen would save considerably if he were in that employment.' But even this testimonial was unavailing, and the office of Comptroller remained empty until Vanbrugh's reinstatement, after George I's accession, in January 1715.

Archer's known letters are not numerous. In the British Museum there is one to Sir Hans Sloane, dated July 15, 1715, in which he asks whether Sloane had 'a designe of selling to builders the ground that looks on the Thames, now the Garden to the School at Chelsey, and at how much a foot and what is the Depth you allow the Ground to be. The person for whom I ask this question,' he adds, 'would put your ground in such reputation that the rest would be soon built.'[2] Also in the British Museum are four consecutive letters from Archer to the nobleman who is best remembered as the Earl of Strafford,

[1] Historical Manuscripts Commission, *Manuscripts of the Marquis of Bath at Longleat*, Vol. I, p. 231.

[2] Add. MSS. 4044. f. 80. Mr Brian Leather has put forward an ingenious suggestion founded on this letter, for which see below, p. 42.

together with copies of Strafford's replies and of the letter from him that started the correspondence.[1] The last-mentioned is dated from The Hague, April 17, 1714,[2] and begins as follows

Sir
upon what you told me at Windsor I sent to Mr London, and had he not died as he did I had certainly got the plan of my gallery at Stainborough but not having nobody at London, that knows it unless you'l be so kind one day as you go to the park through Spring Garden, to call upon his widow, and look over his plans, to find out that of my Gallery, which I shall take as a particular obligation, and if you think fit my Brother will be glad to wait on you thither. I should not have given you the trouble of this letter but that upon your encouragment for building I am resolv'd to try to make an addition to my house in St James's Square,[3] and therefore take the liberty of inclosing these plans to you, they are not done exact enough to be sent to such a master as you are but are sufficient to show you my intention of having a Gallery, and a great room at the end of it, or else having as you see by letter (a) a Pavillion at the end of the Gallery with a room not altogether so large as that in letter B . . .

Strafford goes on to discuss the details of his design and, after remarking that 'when once one is in the morter one can never get out', writes:

The discourse I had with you relating to my building at Stainborough encouraged me to give you this trouble and it would be inexcusable having had so fair an opertunity of consulting the greatest master of that art in Europe should I undertake anything without doing it . . .

Two interesting facts emerge from this letter; first that Archer had been consulted by Strafford at Stainborough, or Wentworth Castle, Yorkshire, and secondly that the plan of the great gallery

[1] Add. MSS: 31, 141. ff. 1550–169.

[2] In England, which still used the Julian or Old Style calendar, it was April 6.

[3] No 5, in the north-east corner. (See A. I. Dasent, *The History of St James's Square*, p. 56). Strafford's house was rebuilt by Brettingham for the fourth earl in 1748.

at Stainborough had for some reason been left in the hands of George London the gardener (who died in 1713).[1] Archer's reply, which is dated April 20, may be quoted in full:

My Lord

The favour of your Lordship's Letter I had acknolledged sooner but for the Latter part relating to the building, of which I was willing to give the most judicious account I could since your Lordship was pleased to ask my poor Opinion, and to pass so many compliments with such high encomiums on me.

The Plan your Lordship sent I perfectly understand in all its parts, and were the Ground on all sides limited and never to be come at, either I should not build at all, or I should build something very near that forme, the greatest objections would be the narroweness of the Galery by which it would very much resemble a passage, and the Darkening the great room at the End of it, and it would be hard, by building on that side of the Garden, to overcome these Difficulties, but by good fortune as soon as I saw the Plan I put Mr Wentworth and Mr West upon enquiry after the Stables that lie on the other Side of the garden, and your Lordship's Steward this post will give you a fair prospect of buying that ground at an easy rate, this purchase will make it much an easier task to contrive a hansome appartement with a Galery, or a Galery with a Pavillion at the end as your Lordship's good tast will not disapprove. If in the meane time you have a desire to see what I can make out of the present ground Ill send you my thoughts upon it; As to Mr Londons affaire I have promised Mr Wentworth to wait on him, if he will obtaine leave from Mrs London, and to view the Drafts in order to find your Lordship's own and if she will not give leave I will speak to Mr Hever the Executor about them, 'tis so barbarous a thing to conceal the Draft, that if I cannot help you to it without appearing openly in it I will even doe that to serve you.

I hope this taking care of your house in Town bespeaks your Lordship's speedy return among us, and that I may have from

[1] The south front of Stainborough was designed for Raby by Johann von Bodt or Bott, for whom see Thieme-Becker, also A. P. S. *Dictionary*. There is an engraving of this front dated 1713, inscribed 'C. Holzendorf Delineavit'. Holzendorf was secretary to the British Embassy in Berlin at the time.

thence occasion of shewing the respect with which I am

> My Lord
> Your Lordships most
> obed: hum: Servt
> Tho: Archer

I beg the favour of your Lordship to present my most hum: Service to my Lady:

In his next letter, dated June 28, 1714, Archer urges Strafford not to build until he had obtained the remainder of the lease of his new ground 'after lady Dover'; 'and till that be don I should wait with patience, for as to the proposall of building a great room partly over the Kitching the rest over the Coach houses, that would crowd and darken the Garden front of the house still more'. On July 9 he sends his plan ('divided into two, because the present ground your Lordship has got goes no further than the first paper'.) In the course of the letter accompanying it he says: 'I thought the Upwright would be of no Service till the Ground plott is approved'. But it never was approved, for on August 3 Strafford wrote that it was 'too great an undertaking for me being in the first place I must loose all my Stables and Coach Houses . . . and my next Objection is, that I would not give a farthing for a Gallery above Stairs, of which I should have but little Injoyment, for then the Ladys would take intire Possession'.

The last letter from Archer in this correspondence is dated, on August 8, 1714, from Tathwell, Lincolnshire. This was the home of his second wife, Ann, daughter of John Chaplin of Tathwell Hall. In the following year, 1715, Archer bought the manor of Hale, near Fordingbridge, Hampshire, where he proceeded to rebuild both the house and the church,[1] (pp. 76, 77) to enclose a highway and a footpath,[2] and doubtless to do many of the other things expected of a country gentleman of that age. This purchase may have been encouraged, and certainly must have been facilitated,

[1] Monumental inscription at Hale.
[2] Warrant in British Museum, Add. MS: 36, 125. f. 3.

by his appointment the same year to the Comptrollership of the Customs at Newcastle-upon-Tyne,[1] which had as its 'member ports' Shields, Sunderland, Hartlepool, Stockton and Whitby. This was not an onerous post. Although the farming out of the Customs was ended in England in 1671, 'the extraordinary system of having one set of officers to do the actual work, and another set of officers who were merely pensioners upon maritime trade, continued for more than a century',[2] and Archer was one of those pensioners.[3]

After 1715 Archer seems to have played little part in public life, though he was Groom Porter to both of the first two Georges. Perhaps we should picture him spending more and more time on his country estate—a supposition which accounts for the design of St John's, Westminster, being altered in execution without his knowledge. In 1739 he set up in Hale church a monument to his two wives and himself. And in 1743—on May 22 according to his epitaph, on May 23 according to the *Gentleman's Magazine*—he died in his house in Whitehall. He was buried at Hale on June 5.[4]

The *Gentleman's Magazine* put Archer's fortune at 'above 100,000 *l*,' and this does not seem an excessive estimate in view of the evidence of his will.[5] For this shows that in addition to Hale he had considerable property in Dorset, Warwickshire and Worcestershire (the latter including the large country mansion called Weathercock or Weatheroak Hall, near Alvechurch), and in London in Grosvenor Square, Bond Street, Duke Street, Pedley Street and Cross Street 'and elsewhere in the County of Middlesex'. On his wife Ann (who outlived him by twelve years) he settled £700 per

[1] Monumental inscription at Hale.

[2] H. Alton and H. H. Holland, *The King's Customs*, p. 105.

[3] There is a minute recording the appointment of 'Robert Daniel to be Mr Archer's deputy as Comptroller of Customs in the port of Sunderland, instead of Thomas Alcock, and at the same allowances' printed in *Calendar of Treasury Books and Papers*, 1735–1738, p. 513.

[4] Hale church register.

[5] P. C. C. 146 Boycott. There is an office copy among the Archer papers from Umberslade at Shakespeare's birthplace, Stratford-on-Avon.

annum, payable from the Hale estate; nearly everything else went to his nephew Henry,

> but it is my express Will and Desire that my said Manor House at Hale and all my Estate Lands Tenements and Hereditaments at Hale South Charford North Charford and Woodfalls should continue and remain for ever in the Name Blood and Family of the Archers and therefore if my said Nephew Henry Archer or any other person or persons to whom the same may at any time hereafter shall ever be so ungrateful to me as to contract or agree to sell or alien the same or any part thereof then and in such Case I give and bequeath the Sum of fifteen Thousand five hundred pounds unto the Hospital for Foundling Children in London to be paid one Month next after the Execution of any Deed or Contract for the Sale or Alienation thereof . . .

Another conditional bequest to the Foundling Hospital was £200 when it should be in a position to keep 400 children. A codicil added six days before Archer's death revokes a legacy of £300 to his nephew Sir Archer Croft 'whose great Misbehaviour and ill Conduct has since rendered him undeserving of any such Esteem and Regard from me', and a second codicil two days later requires that the body of his first wife Eleanor should be taken from Welford to Hale within a month of the death of his widow, 'in a Hearse with six Horses'.

Archer's epitaph insists on his handsomeness as a young man ('eximia Corporis forma Insignis . . . Juvenum Pulcherrimus, Flos, ac Decus'). His only known portrait is the effigy on his monument; this shows a face of which the most marked characteristic, I would say, is alertness, while its Roman cast cannot be altogether due to the sculptor's idealization. Of his character we know nothing more than can be deduced from the facts of his life, his letters, and his works. To his artistic talents he evidently joined qualities that belong to the successful man of affairs; at the same time he possessed his share of that prudence which was inherent in the Archers' attitude to life—and it was mainly this, perhaps, which prevented him from making a greater mark in the pages of political history.

II

DOCUMENTED WORKS

ARCHER's earliest authenticated work is the *north wing of Chatsworth*, Derbyshire (p. 49). Formerly the whole of the pre-nineteenth-century part of this vast house was attributed to Talman, on the strength of Colen Campbell's statement in *Vitruvius Britannicus*, and it was left to Mr Francis Thompson to get at the truth of the matter. The old north wing, according to Mr Thompson, was demolished by Lady Day 1705, and it may be presumed that the new one was begun almost immediately, since the agreement for the stone carving on the façade is dated September 28, 1705:

> Samuel Watson doth hereby Covenant bargain and agree to Carve in Stone Six Corinthean Capitalls for the North Front of Chatsworth House according to a Designe approved on by his Grace [the Duke of Devonshire] at the Rate of five pounds apiece the Stone to be ready masoned as his Graces Charge. And the said Samuell Watson doth hereby further agree to Carve the Modillians and Roses in the Intabliture of the North front, every Modillian and a Rose at the Rate of Ten shillings both together, and to performe the worke, after the best Manner, according to the Designe drawne by Mr Archer.

At some period during the earlier stages of the erection of the front Archer visited Chatsworth, for the housekeeper's accounts for the year ending Michaelmas 1705 contains the item of eleven tons of coals 'to Aire the House for Mr Archer',[1] whose name appears again in a letter from the Duke's steward written in April 1706.[2]

---

[1] Francis Thompson, *A History of Chatsworth*, p. 77.
[2] Ibid., p. 78.

Watson's bill for the stone carving was rendered in March 1707.[1]

Archer's wing at Chatsworth, the main apartment in which was the kitchen, was remodelled in the 1820s by Jeffrey Wyatville, when the main entrance was transferred to this side of the house. The bowed plan (designed to conceal the non-alignment of the north ends of the already completed east and west sides of the house) was retained, but the façade was much altered in detail. Originally the pilasters were rusticated, as a sketch in Wyatville's working notebook, preserved at Chatsworth, shows. Another Wyatville drawing, showing one of his proposed treatments for the front, gives the form of the windows as Archer left them—arched on the two principal floors and oval above. A pencil sketch design for the oval windows, pretty certainly by Archer himself, was preserved by Samuel Watson and is now at Chatsworth, pasted in his *Accounts, Estimates and Designs* with two alternative windows and a shell (title-page, and p. 49). Granted that they are his, these four sketches show that Archer could use a pencil with facility and —as one might expect from his architecture—a certain *bravura*.

The date of *Heythrop Hall*, Oxfordshire (pp. 50-52), is given by Woolfe and Gandon in their continuation of *Vitruvius Britannicus* (to which we also owe all our knowledge of its original plan) as *circa* 1705. The Duke of Shrewsbury, for whom the house was built, was abroad from 1700 till January 1706; the works may equally well have been begun during his absence or shortly after his return. While abroad he kept a diary, and under the date March 13, 1704, occurs the entry:

> Sig. P. Falconieri's *valet de chambre* brought me the draft he had corrected for Whitehall, and one for a house for me. Two or three days ago his master kindly remembered me, and ordered him to put them in my hands; he was then near expiry, and he died this 13th of March, about 24 hour, Italian.[2]

[1] Ibid.

[2] Historical Manuscripts Commission, *Report on the Manuscripts of the Duke of Buccleugh . . . at Montagu House*, Vol. II, p. 776.

This Falconieri must have been Paolo Falconieri, of whom Thieme-Becker gives some account; he was Chamberlain to the Grand Duke Cosimo III of Tuscany and an amateur architect, one of his unrealized projects being an extension to the Pitti Palace. It is not at all unlikely that the draft for a house referred to by Shrewsbury was intended for Heythrop, and that Archer based his own design for Heythrop upon it.

For it can be taken as quite certain that Archer was the architect responsible for the building of the house. Walpole says so in his *Visits to Seats* and both Shrewsbury's recommendation of him for the Comptrollership of the Works and Archer's own reference to work for Shrewsbury in his own application for that post indicate the same thing. If we look for evidence of Archer having used a design by Falconieri we may find it in the plan. Blomfield found fault with Vanbrugh for the smallness of the rooms in his vast palaces, but it is at least possible that Vanbrugh took into account the English climate. This the designer of Heythrop can hardly be said to have done—for the hall measured 32 ft. by 27 ft. (or practically the same as the grand salon at Castle Howard), while the larger drawing room was 47 ft. by 25 ft. and the gallery no less than 81 ft. by 21 ft.

Two exterior details of Heythrop provide important clues to other possible works by Archer. One is the window common to the principal floor of the entrance front and the outer parts of the garden front; this derives from Bernini's Palazzo Chigi (now Odescalchi), in Rome (p. 96). The other is a window remaining at the north-east end of the house (and no doubt originally repeated at the south-west end) which is surmounted by a cleft pediment with its two curved halves turned inside out—another Berninesque motif.

Something of the progress of the works at Heythrop may be learnt from Vanbrugh's letters. In July 1708 Vanbrugh wrote to the Earl of Manchester: 'The Duke of Shrewsbury's house will be About half up this Season',[1] and in November 1709 he tells the

---

[1] Geoffrey Webb (editor), *The Letters of Sir John Vanbrugh*, p. 24.

Duchess of Marlborough: 'There is none of the Roof yet upon [the Duke and Duchess of Shrewsbury's] house, and twil be with great Difficulty if they get it on this Season'.[1] As late as April 1716, writing to the Duke of Marlborough about the possibility of getting stone from Shrewsbury, Vanbrugh mentions 'the danger of the Quarry failing before all be done in his building', though he adds that 'the bulky part of the building is over'.[2] In 1831 Heythrop was gutted by fire, and for forty years after stood derelict. In the rebuilding after 1870 the two main fronts were preserved unaltered, although the interior was entirely remodelled and the service pavilions were rebuilt. An account of the interior as it was early in the nineteenth century is given in Neale's *Views of Seats*. Heythrop is now a Jesuit College.

St Philip's, Birmingham (pp. 53-55), now the Cathedral but by origin the church of one of the very few new parishes to be created in the eighteenth century, was built under an Act of Parliament of 1708. Thomas Archer was one of the board of Commissioners consisting of local gentry appointed to oversee the building of the church; so was his elder brother Andrew, from whose estate came some of the stone and much if not all of the timber. The minutes of the meetings of the Commissioners have been preserved. They show that Thomas Archer attended only one meeting—in August 1709, when it is to be presumed he presented his design. The minute book also contains several agreements with tradesmen. The mason who undertook the stonework was Joseph Pedley, who in March 1710 agreed 'to do the plain of the Stone-Work for $2\frac{1}{2}$ per foot, and the Moldings at 7*d*. per foot; but if the Commissioners find that 7*d*. per foot, for the said Moldings, be not enough, they to give Something more'. In the event the Commissioners did find that 7*d*. per foot for the mouldings was not enough, and in February 1713 it was ordered that Pedley be paid 'the Sum of Six and Thirty Pounds in Con-

[1] Ibid., p. 38.
[2] Ibid., p. 64.

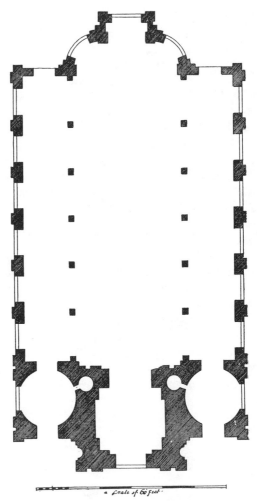

a scale of 60 feet

St Philip's, Birmingham: plan

sideration of his hard bargain made with the Commissioners the 7th day of March 1709 [i.e. 1709/10]'. But it seems that Pedley was still not satisfied, for forty years later the poet William Shenstone, for whom he had carved an urn at the Leasows, wrote to recommend him to Lady Luxborough in the following terms:

> Pedley is an inoffensive old man, and seems to discover notwithstanding his Infirmities, that He has seen a good deal of the World—And if the *World* be taken in a *Scripture*-Sense, he has seen too *much* of it. He has been a great Sufferer by Undertaking Birmingham new-Church; which was, I think, a *Design* of the late Groom Porters. Certain it is, that he has been a great sufferer by the Groom-porter himself; concerning which he relates a Story not much to the Groom Porter's Honour.[1]

One could wish that Shenstone had gone on to relate that story himself, for the light it might have shed on Archer's character.

Of the other craftsmen employed at St Philip's, Richard Huss the plasterer may be mentioned. William Smith, who may be identified as the elder brother of the better known Francis Smith of Warwick, supervised the delivery of two hundred loads of stone, supplied by William Shakespeare, 'at the pitt, at Rowington Quarry, ready for loading'; he was paid ten pounds 'towards his trouble'. The church was consecrated in October 1715, but the tower was not completed till 1725, when George I contributed £600 towards it. The present chancel was added by J. A. Chatwin in the 1880s; originally there was a shallow apse with Corinthian pilasters flanking the altar.

At *Wrest Park*, Bedfordshire, for the Duke of Kent, Archer built an elaborate *pavilion* (pp. 56-58) at the end of the main canal, lying on the centre axis of the house. Its date is given by Colen Campbell in *Vitruvius Britannicus* as 1709. This is likely to be the date of the design or commencement of the building, since there exists another engraved plan, differing slightly in detail, which is dated 1711;[2] moreover, the decorations of the interior—a *trompe-l'oeuil* archi-

---

[1] Marjorie Williams (editor), *The Letters of William Shenstone*, p. 247.

[2] There is a copy in the British Museum, Maps K.7.11.e.

St Philip's, Birmingham

tectural scheme with painted pilasters and busts in niches—are signed 'Hauduroy pinxit 1712'.[1]

The gardens and park at Wrest were laid out in the formal French manner, and Archer's pavilion differed from most English garden buildings of the eighteenth century in being a formal feature in a direct relationship to the house. Its plan is based on Michel-

[1] First noted by H. B. Leather, *Baroque Inspiration* (typescript in RIBA Library). For more about Hauduroy, see C.H. Collins Baker and M. I. Baker, *The Life and Circumstances of James Brydges, first Duke of Chandos*, pp. 285–6.

angelo's plan for S. Giovanni dei Fiorentini in Rome (p. 58), but the number of apsidal and rectangular projections has been reduced from four of each to three. The design must have ocupied Archer at almost the same time as that of St Philip's, Birmingham, and *Vitruvius Britannicus* shows the surface of its dome modelled and ribbed in the same way as the surface of the dome of the church. Either in execution or later this was altered, but the crowning lanterns of the two buildings are very similar and the design of the entrance doorway is basically the same as that of the west doorways of St Philip's. Apart from its function as a focal point in the gardens, the pavilion was designed to serve for hunting parties and occasional suppers. The 1711 plan shows how the secondary rooms on the various floors were allotted; in addition to kitchen and larder the basement contained a bagnio and a water closet, while there were two bed chambers on the principal floor and two servants' rooms above them.

Roehampton House (pp. 59–61), built for Thomas Cary, was according to *Vitruvius Britannicus* designed by Archer in 1712. The elevation given by Campbell is surmounted by an enormous cleft pediment; whether this was never carried out or was subsequently removed is uncertain. In other respects this front still corresponds with Campbell's plate, but the house was otherwise much altered (and added to) by Sir Edwin Lutyens when it became Queen Mary's Hospital. As originally planned with a large entrance court formed by the service pavilions, the quadrant arcades connecting them to the *corps de logis*, and the undulating walls towards the road, this must have been one of the most attractive of all Archer's works. The middle room on the first floor on the entrance front contains murals attributed to Thornhill.

Cliveden House, Buckinghamshire, was built for the Duke of Buckingham to the design of Captain Wynne òr Wynde *circa* 1670. According to *Vitruvius Britannicus*, Archer added the *service pavilions and the quadrant colonnades* (of the Ionic order) linking them to the

27

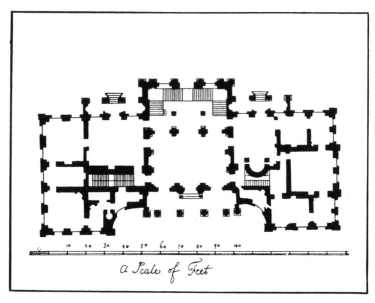

a Scale of Feet

Hurstbourne Priors: superseded plan

main block. Cliveden has been twice burnt since then—in 1795 and in 1849; Archer's additions survived both fires and still do survive, though a good deal altered. Their date is not known.

Hurstbourne Priors, Hampshire (p. 62), was built for John Wallop, who subsequently became Baron Wallop and Viscount Lymington and finally Earl of Portsmouth, after 1712. In the Clarke Collection at Worcester College, Oxford, there is a plan inscribed 'A House designed for Mr Wallop at Husbourne, Hants, by Mr Archer 1712', together with a design for a staircase. This plan does not correspond with the house as built, which was demolished later in the eighteenth century and is now known only through two paintings in the collection of the present Earl of Portsmouth at Farleigh House. But Archer was undoubtedly the designer of this too.

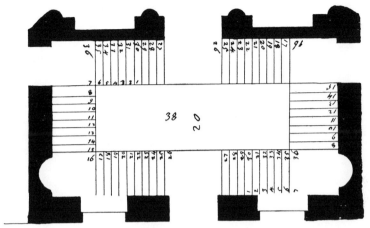

Hurstbourne Priors: design for stairs

St John's, Smith Square, Westminster (pp. 63–68), was the most expensive of the churches built under the Act of Parliament of 1711, its total cost amounting to £40,875.[1] The site was purchased in June 1713, and by the end of 1715 more than £10,000 had been paid to the builders. Yet the church was not consecrated till June 1728, and not opened for public worship till the following November. The masons employed were the partners Edward Tufnell and Edward Strong, with Christopher Cass, and John James (of Greenwich) appears in the accounts as a carpenter with his partner Robert Jelfe. 'Nicholas Hawksmore, Esq' received £9 6s.'for making a Model of a Twisted Column and for his Disbursements for Watching'.

It is said that during the erection of St John's the foundations gave trouble, and that this accounts for certain alterations in the design—more particularly, in the design of the towers. The design

[1] See J. E. Smith, *St John the Evangelist, Westminster: Parochial Memorials,* for a detailed history of the church.

'as it was resolved upon by the Commissioners' was engraved, with an inscription stating that 'the Alterations made since to this Design both as to the Stepps and Pinnacles, were done without the Consent or Knowledge of Mr Archer'. In this engraved design the towers have plain cornices, without modillions, and each is surmounted by a balustrade and two pinnacles; each pinnacle consists of two Corinthian pillars, with an arch between, astride the balustrade, supporting an entablature on which rests a pyramidal finial with a concave base. The alteration of the steps referred to comprised the substitution of parallel retaining walls for the converging ones proposed by the architect. In addition—though this modification was surely due to Archer himself—the central feature within the broken pediment is much simpler in the engraving, and lacks the elaborate recessions of the executed design.

St John's is now but the shell of itself, having been gutted by fire in the blitz. The loss is the less in that it had already, all but two hundred years before, suffered in the same way, and in the subsequent reconstruction of the interior the twelve Corinthian columns that supported the ceiling had been omitted.

St Paul's, Deptford (pp. 69-74), another of 'Queen Anne's churches', was built between 1712, when the site was purchased, and 1730, when the building was consecrated. The masons were Edward Strong and Edward Tufnell and Christopher Cass, as at St John's, Westminster, with John Strong; James Ellis and James Hands were the plasterers; and the altar-piece and pulpit were made by the joiner John Gilliam of Greenwich.[1]

There are four original plans of St Paul's, Deptford, in the British Museum,[2] one of them representing an early design with a different treatment of the west end (p. 72). Strong and Tufnell's *Book of Entry for Mason's Work*, in the library of the Royal Institute of British Architects, shows that the design of the windows was

[1] H. M. Colvin, 'Fifty New Churches', *The Architectural Review*, Vol. CVII, p. 196.

[2] Maps, K. XVIII, 18, e–i.

altered in 1714 after work had begun.[1] St Paul's, like St John's, Westminster, breaks completely with the traditional type of English church plan followed by Archer at Birmingham, although the steeple stands conventionally enough at the west end. Seen from outside, the nave is almost square; the interior approximates to the Greek cross form, the spaces between the arms of the cross being filled by vestries and gallery staircases, but is given a sense of direction in spite of its height by the great Corinthian columns, behind which the galleries are kept well back. In the north and south sides of the nave are doorways, approached by elaborate stone staircases. The steeple is clearly derived from Wren's steeple of St Mary-le-Bow, but is of circular plan at all levels; similarly, the semi-circular portico may derive from the transept porches of St Paul's, though the motif goes back to Pietro da Cortona's S Maria della Pace, Rome,[2] and Archer may have come to it independently of Wren. Archer also designed the former *rectory* (p. 69), which was demolished in 1887.

Hale Park, Hampshire (p. 77), which Archer built for himself in or soon after 1715, consists of a main block with stables and service pavilion connected to it by curved passages. In plan, with its spacious staircase hall, the house is quite characteristic, but its general appearance has been greatly altered both indoors and out. The red brick of the walls, originally exposed, is now rendered with Roman cement, and the proportions of the entrance front have been changed by the raising of the level of the forecourt. The garden front is now virtually a work of Henry Holland, who added a canted bay to the centre of it in 1770,[3] though the stone steps with their wrought iron railing date from Archer's time.

Hale Church (p. 76) was added to and modernized by Archer early in his tenure of the manor. The work is dated by a page in the

[1] H. M. Colvin, loc. cit.

[2] See F. Saxl and R. Wittkower, *British Art and the Mediterranean*, p. 47.

[3] See D. Stroud, *Henry Holland.*

31

register headed *Memo*: 'In 1717 That the Church was begun building, that is the addition that Mr Archer builded.' Previously it was a very small medieval building with a chancel of 1632. Archer added the transept and re-faced the rest in ashlar, with Doric pilasters of marked entasis and doorways of forceful baroque design. The roof and windows were altered in the nineteenth century.

Harcourt House, as it was called for the greater part of its existence, stood until 1903 on the west side of Cavendish Square. It was begun in 1722[1] for Robert Benson, Baron Bingley, and was at first known as Bingley House. Archer's design was altered in execution by Edward Wilcox, but was engraved by John Rocque (p. 75). Features of special interest are the capitals to the pilasters with their in-turned volutes, deriving from Borromini, the splayed jambs of the window cases on the first floor, and the bowed balconies.

[1] J. Summerson, *Georgian London*, p. 92.

III

ATTRIBUTED WORKS

Chicheley Hall, Buckinghamshire (p. 78), has been tentatively attributed to Archer by Mr Arthur Oswald.[1] The fabric of the house, which was built for Sir John Chester, may have been completed by 1703, although there are rain-water heads bearing as late a date as 1721. The fenestration of the front illustrated, with arched windows in the central portion, has affinities with the Harcourt House design and several other works to be ascribed to Archer, and so has the management of the pilaster order, which runs through two storeys only.[2] The doorway in the front illustrated is copied from Bernini's doorways (p. 95) in the Chapel of the Holy Crucifix in the Vatican (with the addition of a hood to throw off the rain); the same type of pediment, as has been mentioned, was used by Archer at Heythrop for windows. The house is built in red brick with stone dressings, a combination much favoured by Archer and employed also in the Wrest pavilion, Marlow Place, Chettle House, Roehampton House, and his own house at Hale. If it was designed by him, the *chancel of Chicheley parish church*, as rebuilt by Sir John Chester in 1708 (p. 79), is presumably his too.

Addiscombe House (p. 80), near Croydon in Surrey, was rebuilt for William Draper, son-in-law of John Evelyn (and his successor as Treasurer of the Commission for Greenwich Hospital). Under the

---

[1] *Country Life*, Vol. LXXIX, p. 485.

[2] As Mr Walter Ison has pointed out to me, the up-sweeping of the cornice to the centre finds its nearest English parallel in Bradmore House, Hammersmith (illustrated in L.C.C. Survey of London, Vol. VI, *Hammersmith*).

date June 27, 1702, Evelyn notes in his diary: 'Draper, with his family, came to stay with us, his house at Addiscombe being new-building.' And on July 11, 1703 Evelyn 'went to Addiscombe . . . to see my son-in-law's new house, the outside, to the coving, being such excellent brickwork, based with Portland stone, with the pilasters, windows, and within, that I pronounced it in all the points of good and solid architecture to be one of the very best gentlemen's houses in Surrey, when finished'. Early in the nineteenth century Addiscombe became the Honourable East India Company's Military Seminary; it has since been demolished.

The mason responsible for the stonework at Addiscombe was Edward Strong, as recorded in the memoir of the Strong family in Clutterbuck's *Hertfordshire*. Tradition used to ascribe the design to Vanbrugh, but no one familiar with Archer's work could doubt that he was the architect. The fantastic portico on the west front, with two columns 25 ft. apart and 40 ft. high,[1] could be due to no one else, and other details of this elevation, such as the doorcase and the aprons to the windows, also speak of him. The east front had pilasters only; here the central division was three windows wide, with a round-headed doorway joined in a single composition with an outsize window, surmounted by a segmental pediment, above it. This central portion was flanked by a recessed bay on either side; the outer parts of the façade had pediments similar to those on the west, and the door was approached by a double flight of steps. The largest rooms were the hall (32 ft. by 20 ft.) on the ground floor, and the saloon (35 ft. by 20 ft.) on the first. The saloon and stair-case had decorations attributed to Thornhill.

Monmouth House (frontispiece), which until 1773 occupied part of the south side of Soho Square, is known to us from an engraving in J. T. Smith's *Antiquities of London*; from the same author's *Nolle-kens and his Times* we may learn something about its interior.

---

[1] These dimensions, and the details of the interior, are taken from H. M. Vibart, *Addiscombe, its Heroes and Men of Note.*

Smith, who visited the house when it was in the process of being demolished, says that it was built for the Duke of Monmouth, who was executed in 1685. But everything about the front of Monmouth House as engraved, from the huge cleft pediment and the spacing of the windows down to such details as the modillion cornices and the tapered pilasters in the attic, proclaims Archer the architect. The conclusion is that he rebuilt the house for the Duchess of Monmouth, possibly about the time of that splendour-loving lady's third marriage, to the Earl of Selkirk, in 1703. A survey plan of the cellars, inscribed 'Dutchess of Monmouth', has been published by the Wren Society.[1]

Russell House (p. 81), now 43 King Street, at the north-west corner of Covent Garden, was built *circa* 1704 for the Earl of Orford, better remembered as Admiral Edward Russell, victor of La Hogue. Russell and the Duke of Shrewsbury had been closely associated in the bringing about of the Revolution of 1688 and in other political ventures. That they should employ the same architect is quite to be expected; to compare the front of Russell House with authenticated designs by Archer is to be certain that they did. On Russell's death in 1727 the house passed to Archer's nephew, Lord Archer of Umberslade. Subsequently it went through many vicissitudes, as (*inter alia*) a hotel, the Cave of Harmony, and the second home of the Institute of British Architects. The façade that adds a touch of baroque exuberance to so many eighteenth-century views of the piazza still survives—with an attic storey added and a van entrance in the centre of the front. The interior was described by John Carter in the *Gentleman's Magazine* in 1814;[2] most of the decorations, however, were then of late eighteenth-century date.

The Cascade House at Chatsworth (p. 82) was first attributed to Archer, on stylistic grounds, by Mr John Summerson. And apart from considerations of style, there is the fact that Samuel Watson

[1] Vol. XII, plate 7.
[2] Vol. 84, 2, p. 444.

undertook some of its carved ornaments in the same agreement (dated September 28, 1705) as he undertook the capitals and entablature details for the north front of the house. The ornaments in question were 'Fower Shells in the Crownes of 4 neeches at 14s. apeece. Eight Scrolls 3 foot long by 1 foot at 10s. each. Fower Festoons betweene the Scrolls 3 foot long 15s. each. Fower shells with leaves in the freeze 2 foot 9 inch long 14s. each. For Shells in the Outsides of the freeze 2 foot over 10s. each. The ffrost workes [i.e., the rustication] at 2s. 6d. a foot.' The dolphins flanking the arch and the figure of Fluvius in front of the dome are by Nadauld.[1]

The whole building, including the lead-covered dome and the lantern, is of stone; under the lantern, which resembles those of the Wrest pavilion and St Philip's, Birmingham, is an open aperture. Inside are four shell-headed niches, flanked by foliated scroll brackets supporting the cornice, and the brackets are linked by festoons of fruit and flowers—all features referred to in Watson's agreement.

Hill House, Wrest (p. 84), was first noticed as a work of Archer's by Mr Brian Leather.[2] It formed a conspicuous feature in the gardens to the east of the original house but was demolished in the eighteenth century; for its appearance and plan we must rely on John Rocque's 1735 *Plan and View of the Buildings and Garden at Rest*.[3] Tell-tale details are the doorway with its splayed jambs and the upper storey of windows, which resemble those of the upper storey of the entrance front at Heythrop. The symmetry of the plan and the in-curved walls are also characteristic of Archer, and just as in the pavilion at the end of the canal he adapted a plan by Michelangelo, so here he has used one in Antoine le Pautre's *Oeuvres d'Architecture*; for in all essentials the plan of Hill House follows that of the first floor of the *maison de campagne* which forms the

[1] Francis Thompson, *A History of Chatsworth*, p. 87.

[2] Op. cit.

[3] There is another version of this plan, lacking plans of the individual buildings, dated 1737.

Hill House, Wrest Park: plan

subject of le Pautre's fourth discourse—though with the wings cut off. (Of course the scale is quite different: le Pautre's central space was for carriages.)

Bramham Park, Yorkshire (p. 83), built for Robert Benson (who was to become Baron Bingley) *circa* 1710, is attributed by the Architectural Publication Society's *Dictionary* to Giacomo Leoni, on the strength of Neale's statement that it was designed by an Italian. But there are good reasons for believing that the architect was really Archer. We know that Archer made the original design for Bingley's house in Cavendish Square;[1] we also know that Bingley supervised the building of Strafford's house at Stainborough[2] and that Strafford consulted Archer at Stainborough.[3]

[1] Supra, p. 32.
[2] J. J. Cartwright, *The Wentworth Papers* 1705–39, p. 84.
[3] Supra, p. 15.

37

From this we may conclude that Benson introduced Archer to Raby and that Archer was in Yorkshire at the time in connection with work for Benson at Bramham Park. The general character of the house is quite sufficiently Archerian to be reckoned as further evidence in support of this, and the sloping carriage way up to the front door puts one in mind of Archer's statement that he had designed 'a stair to ascend Windsor Terrace with coaches'.[1] A significant feature in the garden is a terminal incorporating a capital with in-turned volutes.[2] Finally, the statement that the house was designed by an Italian may be explained by the supposition that Archer's design was based on one brought or sent from Italy, as that of Heythrop may have been. Bramham Park was gutted by fire in 1828.

Kingston Maurward, Dorset, was first suggested as a possible work of Archer's by Mr Howard Colvin.[3] The house was built for George Pitt of Stratfieldsaye between 1717 and 1720,[4] and was originally of red brick with dressings of stone. In 1794 it was cased in Portland stone by Morton Pitt, as the result of a visit by George III, who (instead of admiring the building) 'with his well known iteration, did nothing but utter the words, "Brick, Mr Pitt, brick".' More recently it has undergone other alterations, but its original appearance can be made out in a distant view in Hutchins' *Dorset*.[5] It had baluster-like pilasters in the attic storey, boldly rusticated Corinthian pilasters at the angles, a central pediment with a tall arched window breaking up into it, and aprons and large keystones to the windows.

Marlow Place, Buckinghamshire (pp. 86, 87). The discovery of a

[1] Supra, p. 14. The Bramham carriage slope was built to a curved plan and not as shown in *Vitruvius Britannicus*.

[2] Illustrated in *Country Life*, Vol. XVI, p. 458.

[3] In 'The Bastards of Blandford', *The Archaeological Journal*, Vol. CIV, p. 188.

[4] See A. Oswald, *The Country Houses of Dorset*.

[5] 1774 edition, Vol. I, p. 463.

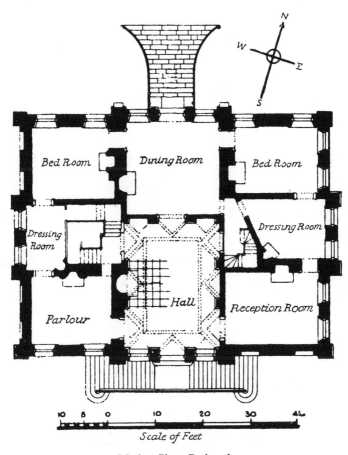

Marlow Place, Bucks: plan

plan by Archer for Hurstbourne Priors puts the attribution of Marlow Place to him beyond all reasonable doubt; for Marlow Place
was built about 1720,[1] for the same John Wallop who was to become the first Earl of Portsmouth. The capitals to the pilasters

[1] For a detailed discussion of the early history of the house see H. M. Colvin,
'The Architectural History of Marlow and its Neighbourhood', *Records of
Buckinghamshire*, Vol. XV.

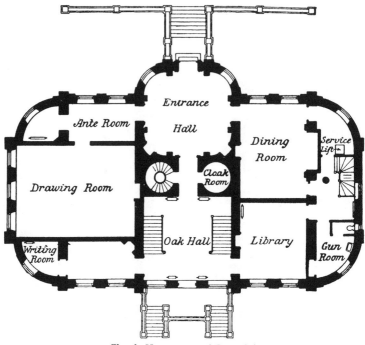

Chettle House: ground floor plan

flanking the central portions of all four fronts are of the Borrominesque type used by Archer in his Harcourt House design, and one of
the main doorways recalls St Philip's, Birmingham, and the Wrest
Pavilion. The capitals at the angles of the house occur, so far as is
known, in only one other English building—the next to be mentioned.

Chettle House, Dorset (pp. 88, 89), was built for George Chafin
circa 1730. The attribution of its design to Archer was suggested by
Professor Geoffrey Webb,[1] who pointed out the resemblance to
Marlow House and the advanced baroque character of the house in

[1] *Country Life*, Vol. LXIV, p. 470.

general. The additional evidence bearing on Marlow House that has since come to light clinches the matter.

The *monument to Susannah Thomas* (who died 1731) in Hampton church, Middlesex (p. 92), was first noticed as pretty certainly a design of Archer by Mr Howard Colvin.[1] In her will Mrs Thomas directed her executors to spend £200 on a monument to herself and her mother—and those executors were Thomas Archer, his wife Ann, and his nephew Henry. The capitals are of the Borrominesque type used by Archer in his Harcourt House design; the form of the arch may be compared with, for instance, the porch of the Wrest pavilion. The monument was executed by W. Powell, who signs it.

The monument at Hale (p. 91) which Archer set up in 1739 to his two wives and himself was also probably made to his own design. A drawing by the sculptor Peter Scheemakers in Sir John Soane's Museum, previously thought to be a preliminary study for this monument, has been found by Mr Rupert Gunnis to correspond with the monument of Sir Christopher Powell at Boughton Monchelsea, Kent.

Other buildings and designs attributed to Archer. In addition to those already discussed, a number of other buildings and designs have been attributed to Archer. Some of these attributions must be disallowed, while others must wait for corroborative evidence before they can rank with those which have been dealt with individually. Both Umberslade Hall and Stoneleigh Abbey belong to the first class.[2] The builder of Umberslade was Francis Smith of Warwick, who may well have designed it too; certainly it has much in common with other works of Smith, and almost nothing in common with any of Archer's. (Accordingly the claims of Newbold Hall,

[1] H. M. Colvin, 'The Bastards of Blandford', *The Archaeological Journal*, Vol. CIV, p. 195.

[2] Umberslade was attributed to Archer in *Wren Society*, Vol. XVII; the south front of Stoneleigh by Muthesius in *Das Englische House* and by the present writer in *The Architectural Review*, Vol. XCIV, p. 127.

attributed to Archer by the editors of the Wren Society's seventeenth volume, must also be dismissed.) As for the south part of Stoneleigh Abbey, this has been conclusively shown to be the design of Francis Smith.[1]

Among the attributions that require the support of further evidence, Mr Brian Leather's suggestion, founded on Archer's letter to Sloane (quoted on page 14), that numbers 4 and 16 Cheyne Walk may have been designed by Archer, deserves first mention.[2] The design of the monument to Archer's father and sister-in-law in Tanworth church (p. 90) has been attributed to the architect, and Mr Hussey has suggested him as the designer of Farleigh House.[3] My own suggestion[4] that his hand may be detected in Mawley Hall and Buntingsdale must be mentioned for the sake of completeness; I am inclined to rate its probability lower than I did. The problem of Beningbrough Hall, Yorkshire, is more important, for this is a house of great distinction.[5] Here we find Bernini's Palazzo Chigi window (p. 96), employed by Archer at Heythrop, forming part of the central feature of a façade; we also find a bold cornice with prominent brackets, such as Archer favoured, and certain interior details may also be held to suggest him.

Finally, a sketch for a doorway, in the Soane Museum, was tentatively attributed to Archer by A. T. Bolton.[6]

[1] By W. A. Thorpe in *The Connoisseur*, December 1946.

[2] Op. cit.

[3] *Country Life*, Vol. XC, p. 478.

[4] *The Architectural Review*, loc. cit.

[5] For an illustrated account see H. A. Tipping and C. Hussey, *English Homes*, Period IV, Vol. II.

[6] *Wren Society*, Vol. XVII, p. 14 and plate 39.

IV

CONCLUSION

ALL ARCHER's known works, together with all those buildings and
designs which to my knowledge have been attributed to him, have
been mentioned in the foregoing pages. What is the general picture
that composes itself after an inspection of them? I said at the begin-
ning that Archer was both the least English and the most baroque
of the four leading architects of the English Baroque, and I must
now attempt to justify this view.

Archer has often been called a pupil of Vanbrugh, but even if one
interprets the term pupil in the loosest possible way there is not
much to give meaning to the phrase. In his churches at Westminster
and Deptford he does, it is true, magnify the elements of design to
a Vanbrugian scale; but the final result is much less static than the
'heroic Baroque' of Vanbrugh. Fundamentally, perhaps the differ-
ence is due to the fact that he was not, as Vanbrugh was, obsessed
by the idea of castle building. As has often been pointed out, there
was a medievalizing tendency in Vanbrugh's work which coloured
much of the English Baroque. But we do not find this in Archer.
Even if we insist on detecting something castle-like in the silhouette
and massing of Chettle, or of the former rectory at Deptford,
the effect is nullified in the building as a whole by the high ratio
of window to wall—a ratio one soon learns to recognize as characteristic of Archer's work. If anything of Archer's is reminiscent of
Vanbrugh, it is the early, markedly Blenheim-like plan for Hurstbourne Priors.

Archer's two London churches have perhaps rather more in
common with Hawksmoor's work. But in his architecture as a

whole there is little evidence of that worship of ancient Rome which inspired so much of Hawksmoor's. What is Roman in Archer is more often modern Roman—of the Rome, that is, which he had no doubt seen in his youth, the Rome of Bernini, Borromini, and the other architects of the seventeenth-century Baroque. And in this he is most un-English—indeed, unique among English architects. It has been said that he must have studied the buildings of the Roman Baroque at first hand, and this may well have been so. But we need not imagine him, in later life, looking out drawings made by himself of the details he had admired. For there were excellent books to which he could refer. The first part of Rossi's *Studio d'Architettura Civile*, published in 1701, contained both the window from Bernini's Palazzo Chigi, which Archer used at Heythrop, and the doorway in the Chapel of the Holy Crucifix in the Vatican, also by Bernini, of which a copy forms the main entrance of the house attributed to him at Chicheley. And the capital with in-turned volutes appeared in many books of engravings illustrating the architecture of seventeenth-century Rome. Like all his more considerable contemporaries, Archer was a bookish architect; in both the garden buildings at Wrest Park attributable to him he started from a plan in a book (though what he built to it was in each case utterly different in general appearance from its prototype.)

But of course it is not by virtue of his imitation of details from Bernini and Borromini that Archer is the most baroque of the architects of the English Baroque. What is most remarkable at Chicheley is not the design of the doorway but the daring and successful use of false perspective in the up-sweeping of the main cornice and parapet so as to give the central part of the front the appearance of much greater projection than it really has. And even if Chicheley Hall was not his, it remains true that no other English architect of the period used curves as freely as Archer did both in his plans and in his elevations, or with so sure a feeling for their potentialities for both illusion and sculptural effect. And no English architect infused more of the essential dynamism of the

Baroque into his work. In Archer's buildings the walls are never mere expanses of dead stone or brick. Indeed, in many of them one is scarcely aware of walls, as walls, at all: instead one's attention is held by what might be described as the extracutaneous skeleton, made up of the classical elements of design, within which they are contained. And in the best of them, such as St John's, Westminster —one of the masterpieces of English architecture—that skeleton is tremendously alive.

Capital with in-turned volutes, from *Opera de Francesco Borromini*. Variants of this capital were used by Borromini in many of his Roman buildings. Capitals of the same kind occur in several of Archer's works, and also in the works of the Bastards of Blandford, who were probably influenced by him. Otherwise they are rare in England; there are examples in the library at Stoneleigh Abbey, Warwickshire (Francis Smith, architect), and in the stair hall at 4 St James's Square.

INDEX

47

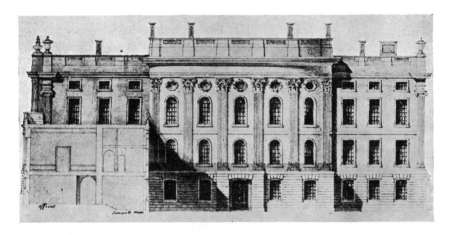

Chatsworth, Derbyshire: a drawing by Wyatville showing the windows as left by Archer.

Sketch design for windows, probably from Archer's own hand, preserved at Chatsworth.

Heythrop Hall, Oxfordshire: the garden front. The terrace is a nineteenth-century addition.

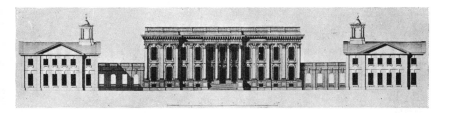

Heythrop Hall: the entrance front. *Above*, from Woolfe and Gandon, *Vitruvius Britannicus*, showing the original pavilions. *Below*, as it exists today.

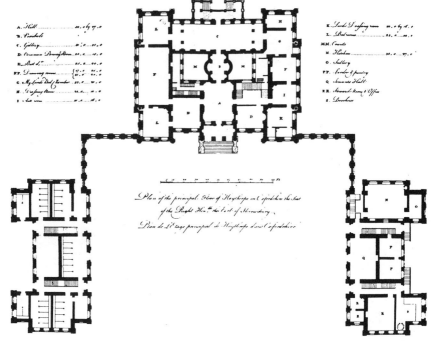

Heythrop Hall: plan from Woolfe and Gandon, *Vitruvius Britannicus*. The apsed vestibule is one of the earliest instances of this kind of planning in an English country house.

St Philip's, Birmingham (now the Cathedral): the steeple.

St Philip's, Birmingham: detail of the east end of the south aisle.

St Philip's, Birmingham: the interior before the addition of the present chancel. From a watercolour in the vestry.

Pavilion at Wrest Park, Bedfordshire: view from the south-west.

Pavilion at Wrest Park: the porch.

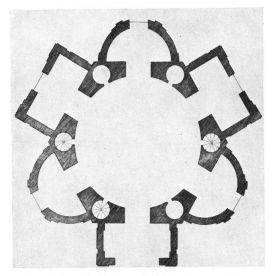

Pavilion at Wrest Park:
plan from Colen Campbell,
Vitruvius Britannicus.

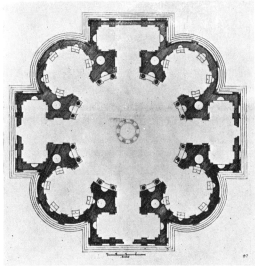

Michelangelo's plan for
S Giovanni dei Fiorentini,
Rome, from J. von Sand-
rart, *Insignium Romae Tem-
plorum Prospectus.*

Roehampton House (now Queen Mary's Hospital), Surrey: the entrance front.

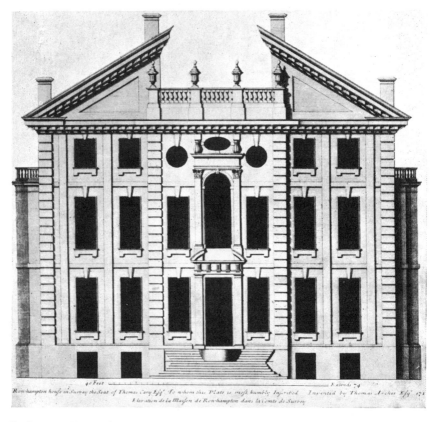

Roehampton House: the entrance front, from Colen Campbell, *Vitruvius Britannicus.*

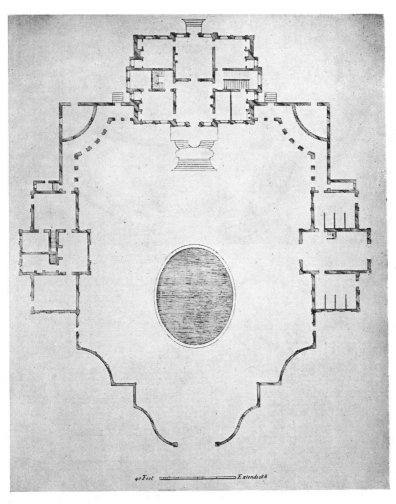

Roehampton House: plan, from *Vitruvius Britannicus*.

61

Hurstbourne Priors, Hampshire: two paintings of the house and grounds in the collection of the Earl of Portsmouth at Farleigh.

St John's, Smith Square, Westminster: from the south-east.

63

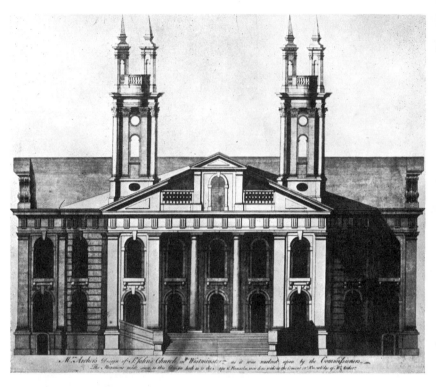

St John's, Westminster: Archer's original design, from an engraving.

St John's, Westminster: the south front as built.

St John's, Westminster: a doorway.

St John's, Westminster: detail of exterior.

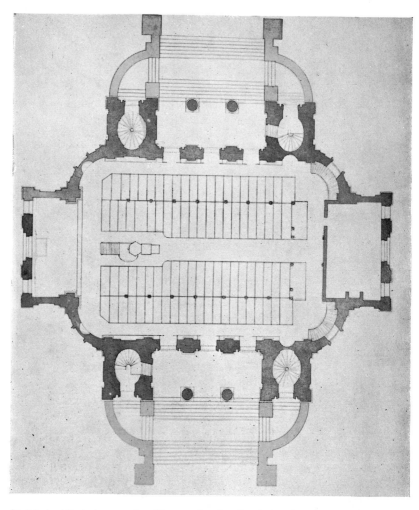

St John's, Westminster: plan. From a drawing by C. R. Cockerell in the Victoria and Albert Museum.

St Paul's, Deptford: an engraving showing the church from the north-west and the rectory (since destroyed) to the south of it.

St Paul's, Deptford: detail of the west front.

St Paul's, Deptford: the nave from the south-east.

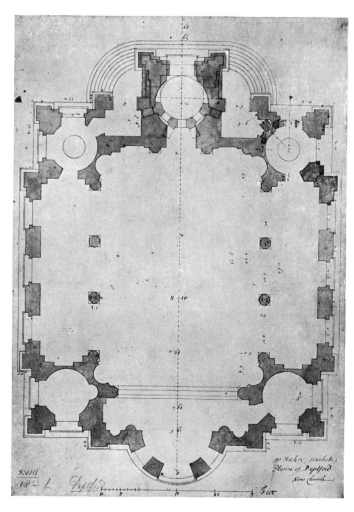

St Paul's, Deptford: a superseded design, showing a different treatment
of the west end. From a drawing in the British Museum.

St Paul's, Deptford: plan of the church as built. From a drawing in the British Museum.

St Paul's, Deptford: the interior, looking south-east.

Harcourt House, Cavendish Square, London: Archer's original design, as engraved by John Rocque.

Hale Church, Hampshire. *Above*, general view from the south-west; the present roof is a nineteenth-century addition. *Below*, the north doorway.

Hale Park, Hampshire, Archer's own country seat. *Above*, the entrance front; *below*, steps on the garden front.

Chicheley Hall, Buckinghamshire: the entrance front.

Chicheley, Buckinghamshire: chancel of the parish church.

79

Addiscombe House, Surrey: the west front. From H. M. Vibart, *Addiscombe, its Heroes and Men of Note*.

Russell House (now 43 King Street), Covent Garden, London: an engraving showing the original state of the front.

Chatsworth, Derbyshire: the Cascade House.

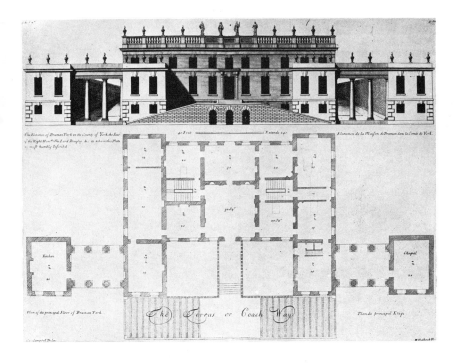

Bramham Park, Yorkshire: plan and elevation from Colen Campbell, *Vitruvius Britannicus.*

Wrest Park, Bedfordshire: Hill House, from a plan of Wrest engraved by John Rocque.

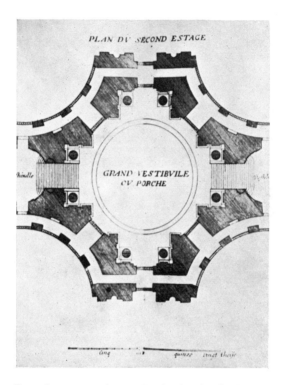

Part of a country house plan in Antoine le Pautre, *Oeuvres d'Architecture*. Compare the plan of Hill House, Wrest, on p. 37.

Marlow Place, Buckinghamshire: the garden front.

Marlow Place, Buckinghamshire: the hall. The mantelpiece is of mid-eighteenth-century date.

Chettle House, Dorset: the entrance front.

Chettle House, Dorset: the staircase hall.

Tanworth-in-Arden, Warwickshire: monument to Thomas Archer senior and Mrs Andrew Archer.

Hale, Hampshire: monument to Thomas Archer the architect
and his two wives.

Hampton, Middlesex: monument to Mrs Susannah Thomas.

Part of a letter from Archer to the Earl of Strafford, relating to the latter's projected gallery in St James's Square. In the British Museum.

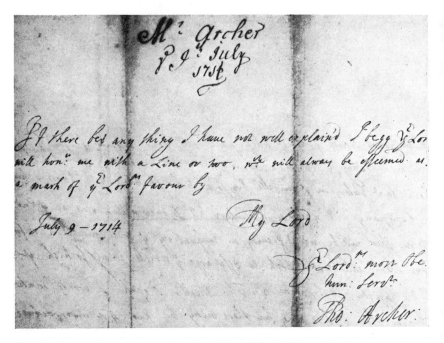

End of the letter from Archer to the Earl of Strafford of which the opening is reproduced on p. 93.

Doorway by Bernini in the Chapel of the Holy Crucifix in the
Vatican, from Rossi, *Studio d'Architettura Civile*. The prototype of
the Chicheley Hall doorway (p. 78) and of a window at Heythrop.

Palazzo Chigi (later Odescalchi), Rome: a detail from Rossi, *Studio d'Architettura Civile*. A window of the design shown was employed by Archer at Heythrop; it also occurs at Beningbrough Hall and in an unexecuted design made for the Duke of Newcastle by William Talman.